Praise for T
Becoming Familiar with Educational
Research to Connect Theory to Practice

MW00986650

"*Teacher as Researcher: Becoming Familiar with Educational Research to Connect Theory to Practice*, written by Smita Guha, is an essential guide for teacher-researchers on writing a master's thesis. Concerned students, teachers, and researchers will learn how to formulate their research questions, articulate the purpose and significance of their study, and find related scholarly published articles. Viewing related literature will help teacher-researchers create a protocol for their own research. This book will also teach researchers how to analyze the results of data and write a discussion on that data."—**Ashok Chakraborty**, adjunct professor, Sacred Heart University, and retired Yale faculty cancer research scientist

"At long last, a comprehensive and reader-friendly guidebook that assists undergraduate, graduate, and even doctoral students in understanding the research process from the inside out. With clarity and focus, Guha guides the reader through the conceptualization of each stage of a study and provides extensive suggestions, resources, websites, forms, and checklists for qualitative, quantitative, mixed-methods, and action research studies. She offers students the support necessary to follow a line of investigation, explore multiple scholarly sources, manage their data, elaborate on their findings/conclusions, and produce their own evidence-based classroom studies that connect theory to practice. *Teacher as Researcher: Becoming Familiar with Educational Research to Connect Theory to Practice* will certainly be one of the recommended texts for my case courses in the Touro Graduate School of Education. Thank you Dr. Guha!"—**Dr. Joanne Robertson-Eletto,** associate professor of education in the master of science in the teaching literacy program, Touro College Graduate School of Education

"*Teacher as Researcher: Becoming Familiar with Educational Research to Connect Theory to Practice* is written by Dr. Smita Guha, a university faculty member who spends time in the real world of classroom teaching, making her approach relevant to actual practice. The text provides the classroom teacher with a concise, easy-to-understand overview of the research process and how it can be incorporated into daily teaching processes without taking away from or lumbering the teacher with tedious and often unnecessary discussion."—**Peter Quinn**, former professor in and chair of the Department of Curriculum and Instruction, School of Education, St. John's University

"As an adjunct professor of education at St John's University who teaches the thesis research course for master's degree recipients, I have long searched for the perfect textbook to introduce to students who have to be engaged in a research project that will inform their work in accomplishing classroom success among their own students. Guha's book achieved what I have been searching for: a compendium that leads the graduate student involved in an action research project.

Teacher as Researcher: Becoming Familiar with Educational Research to Connect Theory to Practice addresses the need for an introductory text that is easy to read and does not bog down the reader with statistical language and methodology. This text serves as a guide for educators involved in a thesis project to examine significant issues and problems in the classroom. It leads the researcher engaged in action research from developing a plan, to organizing a draft that segues to the actual action research itself, to reporting the results.

Guha's book provides the teacher-researcher with a pathway from initial concept to enduring understanding, and from research question to analysis of an action research project. In this manner the researcher can develop a clearly stated research question, make connections to literature reviews with concomitant hypotheses, and conduct the actual research. Incorporated within this structure are ethical considerations in conducting research. Guha provides readers with a rubric—developed at St. John's University—that acts as a road map to the contextual cues needed for a successful project. The attention to detail makes this a landmark text."—**Leonard Golubchick**, adjunct professor, St. John's University, Metropolitan College of New York, and Long Island University Rockland, greater New York City area

"*Teacher as Researcher: Becoming Familiar with Educational Research to Connect Theory to Practice* is a step-by-step guide on educational research that covers such topics as choosing the title, writing the abstract, preparing the literature review, deciding on methodology, preparing qualitative and quantitative studies, collecting and organizing data, analyzing the data, and drawing conclusions. Guha author includes worksheets and sample forms on peer observations, organizing research, evaluating the literature review, rubrics for research, test instruments, and rubrics for case studies. Also included are assignment worksheets for the research process and an extensive bibliography of resources. Guha's book is a helpful and practical resource."—**Lucy Heckman**, associate professor and head of reference, St. John's University Libraries

"This short and concise primer on how to conduct basic research is essential for the novice researcher. Written in words that are clear and understandable, *Teacher as Researcher: Becoming Familiar with Educational Research to Connect Theory to Practice* may be used as an introduction to reading more complex works in action research or case studies. It can also be used as a stand-alone text for beginning researchers, as it gives good examples and homework assignments that will afford preservice and in-service teachers the confidence that they, too, can read and conduct research. Many books on research frighten off the reader with their technical jargon and implicit expectations. Guha's primer breaks that mold."—**Brett Elizabeth Blake**, PhD, professor and senior research fellow, Vincentian Center for Social Justice and Poverty, St. John's University, and coauthor of *Teaching All Children to Read*.

Teacher as Researcher

Teacher as Researcher

Becoming Familiar with Educational Research to Connect Theory to Practice

Smita Guha

Rowman & Littlefield
Lanham • Boulder • New York • London

Published by Rowman & Littlefield
An imprint of The Rowman & Littlefield Publishing Group, Inc.
4501 Forbes Boulevard, Suite 200, Lanham, Maryland 20706
www.rowman.com

6 Tinworth Street, London, SE11 5AL, United Kingdom

British Library Cataloguing in Publication Information Available

Library of Congress Cataloging-in-Publication Data

Names: Guha, Smita, 1965– author.
Title: Teacher as researcher : becoming familiar with educational research
  to connect theory to practice / Smita Guha.
Description: Lanham : Rowman & Littlefield, [2021] | Includes
  bibliographical references and index. | Summary: "Teacher as Researcher
  is a complete guide for teachers involved in a case study or action
  research in their classroom. The purpose of this book is to offer a set
  of research tools for teachers to follow through the inquiry process and
  provide effective solutions to significant problems in their
  classroom"—Provided by publisher.
Identifiers: LCCN 2021020115 | ISBN 9781475862300 (cloth) | ISBN
  9781475862317 (paperback) | ISBN 9781475862324 (epub)
Subjects: LCSH: Action research in education.
Classification: LCC LB1028.24 .G85 2021 | DDC 370.72—dc23
LC record available at https://lccn.loc.gov/2021020115

This book is dedicated to all the teachers who work tirelessly to make a difference in the lives of children.

CONTENTS

CONTENTS

PREFACE

Purpose of This Book

*T*eacher as Researcher: Becoming Familiar with Educational Research to Connect Theory to Practice is written for in-service or preservice teachers involved in research to improve classroom instruction and help students in their learning process. This is a complete guide appropriate for in-service teachers doing research in their classroom or preservice teachers as a guest teacher in a classroom. The purpose of this book is to offer a set of research tools for teachers to follow through the process of inquiry and provide effective solutions to significant problems in their classrooms.

Teacher as Researcher is a step-by-step guide for teachers to get involved in research in the classroom. This book will guide teachers in setting the background of the problem for the study, elaborating on techniques to find related research articles, formulating a research question, stating purpose of the study, indicating need and significance of the study, and designing instruments to triangulate and then collect data. Finally, this book will help teachers analyze the results and discuss the data, as well as write up the research until the point of completion. This book does not include statistical analysis of data or heavy-duty statistics.

Structure of This Book

This book is designed to help teachers target the problems in their own classrooms and inquire about the different strategies that exist to effectively solve the problems. Viewing related literature will help teachers create a stage for their research and test out the strategies in their field.

Teacher as Researcher is a guidebook for teachers as researchers written in a simple, straightforward manner. The simplicity, clarity, and brevity of this book will help teachers conduct an action research study in the classroom or learn to do a case study with their students to help students with the learning process, fostering continuous professional growth for teachers.

Appendix A gives guidelines for writing a literature review, appendix B provides a consent form template, appendix C is a sample survey questionnaire, appendix D gives a research paper outline, appendix E features guidelines for writing a case study on a child, appendix F provides assignments you can follow to complete your research project, and appendix G offers rubrics to help you evaluate your work.

Benefits and Features of This Book

This book will help teachers involved in research. Teachers may be required to do research while completing their master's degree, or they may want to be involved in research to improve their classroom instruction and help children in the learning process.

The Role of the Researcher

This is an inquiry based on teachers' reflection on professional practice. Teachers often confront issues in their classrooms or face challenges with students. It is important for teachers to reflect on their practice and journal their reflections, but that alone may not be sufficient. Teachers need guidance to examine the problem, conduct research from the available literature, and get involved in the process of inquiry.

ACKNOWLEDGMENTS

I acknowledge that there are certain items I have borrowed while I worked with other faculty members in the School of Education during the process of course development. These items are stated in this book only to help the students who are in the teacher education program. Therefore, I would like to thank the School of Education at St. John's University.

I would also like to sincerely thank the editorial team at Rowman & Littlefield, especially Tom Koerner.

Furthermore, I extend my sincere thanks to all the reviewers of this book. All the reviewers have extended their support for this book.

INTRODUCTION

*T*eacher as Researcher: Becoming Familiar with Educational Research to Connect Theory to Practice will help teachers become familiar with educational research and contribute to the continued growth of sensitive, caring, and knowledgeable teachers. It will help teachers connect theory to practice through the development and investigation of a research question grounded on individual interests.

Specifically, this book will focus on preservice or in-service teachers as researchers administering an action research study or case study in their classrooms. It will guide teachers in writing a critical review of related research literature and focus on field testing of the research question.

Overview of Educational Research

What Is Educational Research?

Educational research is a systematic investigation that includes the collection and analysis of data to answer a question in order to contribute to our knowledge about educational theory or practice (McMillan & Wergin, 2010).

Traditional research methods are categorized under three subcategories: quantitative, qualitative, or mixed method. Quantitative research requires collection and analysis of numerical data (e.g., test scores, frequency of participation, attitude scales, etc.). Qualitative research methodology requires narrative data (e.g., observation, interview, open-ended survey questions, journal entries, etc.). Mixed methodology involves both quantitative and qualitative research.

Quantitative research methodologies focus on a deductive approach, which means researchers work from general to specific. A topic is narrowed down to a specific hypothesis that is tested. On the other hand, qualitative research methodologies use inductive reasoning, which means researchers work from specific observations and conclude with broader generalizations. See textbox I.1 for a comparison.

Textbox I.I. Comparison between Quantitative and Qualitative Models

Quantitative Model

1. The quantitative model explains relationships between variables.
2. The research design is predetermined.
3. The researcher is a detached observer.
4. Valid and reliable instruments are required (e.g., tests, surveys, measures of variables, tick sheets).
5. Experimental research is typical.
6. Results are generalizable to other populations.

Qualitative Model

1. Participants explain relationships from their reality.
2. Design emerges in relation to what's most logical.
3. The researcher is immersed.
4. Instruments are not statistically valid or reliable, as they are generally not quantifiable (e.g., observations, interviews, logs, journals, running records).
5. Ethnographic research is typical.
6. Its generalizability is limited to similar settings.

What Is Action Research?

Action research is defined as any systematic inquiry conducted by teachers in the field of teaching, as well as the learning process or environment, for the purpose of gathering information about how they teach and how their students learn (Mills, 2011).

According to Stringer (2014), "Action research is solutions-oriented investigation leading to resolution of issues investigated" (p. 35). Action research is characterized as research done by teachers for themselves, inquiring about their own practice (Johnson, 2008). Therefore, action research allows teachers to study their own classrooms, their own instructional methods, their own students, and their own assessments in order to better understand them and be able to improve and be effective (Mertler, 2017). With action research studies, teachers become lifelong learners.

Models of Action Research

There are numerous models of action research. Some of the models (Mertler, 2017, p. 14) are listed in table I.1:

Table I.I. Action Research Models

Stringer (2007)	"look, think, act"
Lewin (2007)	"fact finding, planning, taking action, evaluating and amending the plan, second action step"
Bachman (2001)	"gather information, plan actions, observe and evaluate actions, reflect and plan for the next spiral cycle"
Riel (2007)	"planning, taking action, collecting evidence, and reflecting"

While these models are important to understand, teachers need to consider the following steps. There are seven steps in an action research study:

1. Identify the problem through repeated observations.

2. Brainstorm all possible solutions, then develop a short list of the solutions after reviewing literature.

3. Implement the solutions: gather information three different ways.

4. Observe and document with date.

5. Analyze the effectiveness of each solution.

6. Reflect and present findings.

7. Repeat the effective solution by taking action.

What Is a Case Study?

A case study is an in-depth qualitative research study of an individual person or group. In order to develop a research question in a case study, you need to think of a "how" or "why" question, which would be the rationale for a case study. The unique strength of a case study is in its depth. It must have a full variety of evidence, such as documents, artifacts, direct observations, and interviews. A case study must have some empirical method and present some empirical (quantitative and qualitative) data (Yin, 2018). Case studies could include single or multiple case studies (Stake, 2006).

Case Study Design Components

There are six main components in designing a case study. They are as follows:

1. Developing the research question.

2. Researching the background of the case.

3. Studying the case itself.

4. Developing the suggested plan of action.

5. Connecting data with the case by matching the pattern and explaining well.

6. Interpreting the data.

The research question in a case study is very important. The question should address "who," "what," "where," "how," and "why." Once you have developed the question, other components flow from one to the other.

The next step is to search literature using a few keywords to narrow down the search. Then select a few studies on the same topic and examine each study carefully. This process may help you stimulate more thinking on how to proceed. Reading more studies on the same topic will help you get a good grasp of how to strengthen your study.

At this point, some development in the theoretical perspective prior to data collection is needed. You could follow a theorist and gather some research studies in the same line. However, existing research may provide some theoretical background that you may further develop. You could plan to develop a single case study or multiple case studies.

If the case is an unusual or an extreme critical case, then it is a single case study (Yin, 2018). When individual case studies predict similar results or contrasting results, then you could develop multiple case studies (Yin, 2018).

Proper data collection methods are critical. If the data are not collected properly, the whole study falls apart. One way to overcome this problem is to do a pilot study. Once the pilot study yields satisfactory results, then you could proceed with a larger scale.

All research conducted must abide by certain research ethics. The school principal and parents of minor or vulnerable children must sign a written consent form. The students should be notified about the purpose of the research before administering any treatment. Further, you must let the participants know that this research process has no effect on their grades, that their participation is optional, and that they can withdraw at any given time without any reason. You as a researcher must avoid any kind of bias (Yin, 2018).

You must check with your university's Institutional Review Board (IRB) about the guidelines to protect human subjects. Refer to the consent form template in appendix B.

Data must be collected from multiple sources to ensure triangulation. The researcher must also maintain a chain of evidence. To converge evidence, the following are some common choices for data collection instruments:

1. Documents

2. Observations (direct or participant)

3. Structured interviews and surveys

4. Open-ended interviews

5. Focused interviews

6. Pictures

7. Videotapes

8. Audio tapes

9. Journals (yours or the students')

10. Surveys

11. Sample of student work (assessments, homework, projects)

12. Conferencing notes and running records

13. Disciplinary reports

14. Meeting minutes

15. Tests and scores

16. Log sheets

17. Peer observations

Table I.2 is a template to help you align your questions with your instruments:

Table I.2. Data Collection Template

Subquestions	Data Source 1: Field Note Journal	Data Source 2: Samples of Student Work	Data Source 3: Conference Notes	Data Source 4: Unit Assessments
1.				
2.				
3.				
4.				

When all these components are fulfilled, you will need to write a case study report. The following are the steps that will help you develop and write the content of your case study report so that it is helpful to readers.

1. Describe the problem and state the research question.

2. Provide relevant background.

3. Describe the solution.

4. Evaluate the response to the solution.

5. Reflect about the problem and the solution.

6. Tell the whole story.

7. Provide recommendations.

Case Study for an Individual Child

A case study is an in-depth look at an individual child. It is often based on both observations of and interviews with the child. In order to provide a comprehensive view of the child's development, teachers must make multiple observations while the child is engaged in various types of activities. Case studies provide a core of information to which theory, research, and experience can be related. Teachers must identify the relevant facts surrounding a situation when they engage in problem solving. At the conclusion, case studies are usually summarized in narrative form to identify the child's strengths and needs, as well as recommendations for continued development.

In general, the typical format of a case study is as follows:

- Background of the problem
- The case about the child with demographic information
  - Physical development
  - Emotional development
  - Cognitive development
  - Social development
- Conclusion with recommendations from the teacher

The following are some tips that can help you write up the case study:

Interview teachers and other individuals associated with the child.

Find or develop a checklist about the particular aspect of child development that you are focusing on and then pilot test the checklist at least three times with three different children to examine the appropriateness of the checklist.

Gather a portfolio of the student's work samples.

Observe the student in various situations and interacting with different adults and children.

Write a progress report.

Experimental research has two groups of participants. One of the groups is called a control group, and the other group is the treatment group. During the study period, the control group receives no treatment, and the treatment group receives all the treatments. You may do a pre-test and post-test before and after to examine the effectiveness of the treatments. You want to see that the treatment group does better in the post-test as opposed to the control group.

As a teacher, you can be an active researcher to improve your instruction. Table I.3 will give you an idea of the steps to follow in organizing an experimental research, an action research, or a case study.

Table I.3. Outline for Organizing Research

Experimental Research	Action Research	Case Study
Introduction	Identifying problem	Objective
Literature review	Literature review	Literature review
Methodology	Methodology	Methodology
Results	Findings	Analysis
Discussion and conclusion	Conclusion and take action again	Conclusion and recommendation

Connecting Theory to Practice

Research is used to develop theories that help determine best practices in education (Johnson, 2008). These best practices help teachers create effective experiences for the students (Johnson, 2008). Therefore, it is important to connect theory to practice.

Research needs to be integrated with the teacher's daily schedule and should be written in simple, clear language that is easy to follow. The research should be practical and relevant to the needs of the teachers. The teacher, therefore, needs to be actively involved in the research process. Parsons and Brown (2002) state that "teaching decisions are not only shaped by theory and research, but in turn help give shape and new directions to educational theory and research" (p. 7).

The theory behind the practice in an action research study is different from quantitative research. The main outcome of an action research study is to resolve the problem in the classroom where the study is focused.

This book is about the teacher as researcher and will focus mainly on action research and case study.

Discussion Questions

1. What are the different types of research studies?

2. What is an action research study?

3. What are the steps of developing an action research study?

4. What is a case study?

5. What are the steps of developing a case study?

6. What is ethics in research?

7. Why is it important to abide by ethics in research?

Activities

1. Find an action research study in your subject area.

2. Find a case study in your subject area.

3. Compare an action research study and a case study.

CHAPTER ONE
GETTING STARTED

Overview of the Research Project

Whether you are a preservice or in-service teacher, the first step is to brainstorm some of the areas you are interested in or where you are having issues in your classroom. After selecting a topic of interest, you should search articles relevant to your topic to find out what exists in this subject area. The literature review must be based on key terms of your topic of interest. Then you need to narrow down your topic and come up with a research question. After selecting and refining a research question, search the literature again to make sure you have selected the important articles related to your topic.

You will coin themes, group the research articles under each theme, compare and contrast main points of the articles, synthesize, and write the review of literature. At that point, you may refine the research question if needed. Following the research question, you will write down the purpose and research hypothesis.

Now you are ready to move forward with the methodology section. First comes the *setting*, which could be the school where you are teaching, and then the *subject*, which would be your students if you are doing an action research project. Find from the existing

1

research the type of *instruments* that other authors have used in the past. Then you will decide on the test instruments. After that, you need to decide on the *procedure*, which is the *method of data collection*. Then you will decide on the *method of data analysis*.

You are then ready to do the *field testing*, where you examine your research question and find the answers with the help of the test instruments. Once you have finished collecting data, then you need to write down the *results* of your research.

The next important item is the discussion, where you need to discuss the results from your data in simple terms to tell the general audience. You should also mention the *implication of your study*. You also need to address your data and align it with the data of the related literature. This is where you identify the *limitation* of your research and suggest *ideas of future research*. Lastly you write the conclusion where you state the purpose of the study detail the findings, and, finally, restate the importance of the study.

∼

The following are some YouTube videos that will provide a background.

- What is educational research?
  https://www.youtube.com/watch?v=5ucLcy_3jZo

- Qualitative versus quantitative research
  https://www.youtube.com/watch?v=69qP8kFJp_k

- Action research
  https://www.youtube.com/watch?v=Ov3F3pdhNkk

- What is a good action research question?
  https://www.youtube.com/watch?v=LWLYCYeCFak
  https://www.youtube.com/watch?v=71-GucBaM8U

- AD/HD Case Study (ER)
  https://www.youtube.com/watch?v=1LHDB-vv4mU

Developing a Good Action Research Question

A good action research question should be important and meaningful to you as a teacher-researcher. The question should be relevant to your personal and professional growth. You should have passion, energy, and commitment to the action research project. it should impact you intellectually and affectively.

Ideas for a Good Action Research Question

1. The research question is important: A research question should focus on teaching and learning practices. It should have an impact on students' behavior or achievement. *Example:* What can I do to encourage students to actively participate in my class discussion?

2. The research question is manageable within the time constraints of the researcher. It should not be too broad to answer, nor should it be too narrow that it cannot offer much insight.

   Example of a question that could be too narrow: What can I do to stop students from talking in class?

3. The research question is contextual. The question should be embedded in the day-to-day work of the researcher rather than an extra project added on to existing teaching tasks.

   Example: What motivational strategies can I employ to increase the achievement of girls in science who are failing in elementary grades?

Six Phases of Action Research

- Phase 1: Identify the problem.
- Phase 2: Develop the research question.

- Phase 3: Develop a plan of action. Brainstorm solutions and narrow down on a few solutions that are manageable and practical.

- Phase 4: Collect data to ensure triangulation.

- Phase 5: Analyze data.

- Phase 6: Plan for future action.

Helpful Websites Related to Action Research
https://sdawp.ucsd.edu/resources/teacher-research/index
.html
https://www.edutopia.org/article/how-teachers-can-learn
-through-action-research
https://www.naeyc.org/resources/pubs/vop/about-teacher
-research
http://www.aral.com.au/resources/index.html
http://rubble.heppell.net/TforT/default.html
http://www.brown.edu/academics/education-alliance/
publications/action-research
http://www.emtech.net/actionresearch.htm

Helpful Websites for Case Studies
https://www.bu.edu/ctl/teaching-resources/using-case
-studies-to-teach/
https://www.edutopia.org/article/making-learning-relevant
-case-studies

Table 1.1 will help you develop your research plan.

Table 1.1. Developing a Research Plan

1. My research topic is:
2. The purpose of my study is:
3. My research question(s) is/are:
4. Important demographic variables include:
5. The instruments needed to answer my research question are:
6. The following must be considered in my data collection process in order to answer my question:
7. The most appropriate type of data to collect for my study is:
   - quantitative
   - qualitative
   - mixed
8. The specific data I will collect are:
9. My research design can be best described as (explain why):
10. I will code, organize, and analyze data by using
    - highlighters
    - "sticky notes"
    - other
11. I will analyze my data using:
12. I will present my data
    - in narrative form
    - in narrative form using tables and graphs
13. A summary of my research finding includes (use bullet form):
14. Something I learned from my study was:
15. Limitations of my study include:
16. Recommendations for changes in my teaching include:
17. Recommendations for the future include:

Discussion Questions

1. How would you get started on a research project?

2. What are the steps in a research study that researchers need to follow?

3. How should you develop a good action research question?

4. What are the phases of developing an action research project?

5. What are your views of doing research in your classroom?

6. What are your ideas in getting started with a research project?

7. Why do you want to get started with an action research study or a case study?

Activities

1. Find an action research study in your subject area and write down the steps that the author followed. You may use a graphic organizer to do this activity.

2. Find a case study in your subject area and write down the steps that the author followed. You may use a graphic organizer to do this activity.

CHAPTER TWO
WRITING THE TITLE FOR YOUR STUDY

The title of the research study is very important. The title should be considered thoughtfully so that it captures the attention of the readers. The title should be comprehensive so that it has all the essentials of the study. You may want to include the topic, the subject area, and the sample characteristics. For example, the title "Technology Usage in the Math Classroom" gives readers some idea about the study, but there is room to insert important information. The title suggests that the study is about "using technology" and the "math classroom," but qualifiers can be added, such as "elementary classroom" or "secondary classroom." The word *examining* or *investigating* could be added at the beginning as well.

However, a lengthy title with a lot of words might not grab the reader's attention. My suggestion is to give your title some thought and check for clarity and comprehensiveness. It is now your turn to write a tentative title of your study. Play around with some of the keywords on the topic, look for keywords in a related study you have examined, or look at the subject descriptors among the related studies to consider the title of your study.

It is advisable to write down the titles that you are considering and check with a couple of people who are not familiar with your study to find out if from the title the readers could tell you what the study will be about. Take a vote and then revise the title. Toward the completion of your study, revisit the title to determine whether the title is appropriate or needs to be revised or fine-tuned. Your title should have no more than 15 words.

Discussion Questions

1. Why is the title important in a research study?

2. How would you create a title for your research study?

Activities

1. Find some research articles and examine the titles.

2. From the titles of each article, what can you tell about the content of the article?

3. To what extent does the title of an article create an impact on the reader?

For Your Study

1. Write the title for your study.

WRITING THE
ABSTRACT FOR YOUR STUDY

The abstract should be written toward the end of your study. You may write some of the key terms that need to be addressed in the abstract at the beginning of your study and then complete at the end of the study. The abstract should be written in a very straightforward and direct manner. You can state the goal, objective, and purpose of the study. You can also include the characteristics of the sample or the setting of your study Finally, you need to include the important points from the results of your study. Perhaps you can also include the significance or the importance of the study. Usually, the abstract is roughly 120 words and is italicized. If you are planning to send your study for publication, you need to check with the guidelines of each publication.

Discussion Questions

1. What is the purpose of writing an abstract for a study?

2. Why should you write the abstract at the end of your study?

Activities

1. Find two research articles and critically examine the abstracts.

2. Compare and contrast the main points of the abstracts of each article.

For Your Study

1. Write the abstract for your study.

CHAPTER FOUR
WRITING THE
INTRODUCTION FOR YOUR STUDY

Writing an introduction is an art. This is the first part of your study where you are sharing your research with the readers. You should write the introduction in such a way that it catches the attention of the readers from the first line. In order to capture the attention of your readers, you must state an important problem that needs to be addressed. You can also mention whether—and if so, how—newspapers or other media have focused on the problem. Then you can expand with a couple of sentences about the problem to determine the seriousness of the study.

The introduction should end with the purpose of the study. The readers, then, will get a clear idea of the focus of the study and will determine if they want to proceed reading the study. Usually, the introduction is one long paragraph. The introduction should flow naturally into the background of the problem, which is the next phase of your study.

Discussion Questions

1. How do you think an author should write the introduction to a research study?

2. How is an introduction in a research study similar and different from any other form of writing?

Activities

1. Find a couple of research studies in your subject area and examine the introductions.

2. Create the fields (e.g., purpose, research question, sample, etc.) from the two research studies that you are reviewing.

For Your Study

1. Write the introduction for your study.

WRITING THE BACKGROUND OF THE PROBLEM FOR YOUR STUDY

T he background of the problem should connect to the introduction of your study. This section is the foundation of your study. Therefore, it is very important to highlight all the problems associated with the topic that your study addresses, from general to specific. The background of the problem of your study has to be detailed enough so that the readers have a clear understanding of the problem area and are interested to read further.

The background of the problem of your study should comprise a few paragraphs detailing the complete picture of the problem, the importance of the problem, and the major concerns associated with the problem. This area should be written in detail and should be convincing enough so that the readers feel concerned that this is a serious problem. This section clearly sets the stage for your study. By pointing to the seriousness of the problem and the issues that are associated with it, you are setting the tone of your study. The tone of this section could be a persuasive one that will compel the readers to focus on this topic and, ultimately, will induce them to read your study.

In the case of an action research study, you can discuss the problems that you are having in your classroom. While the problem could be with a particular student, it also could be with a group of students or about classroom instruction. For example, if your students don't visit the reading area in your classroom or if a group of students shows no interest in a subject area, you can think of developing an action research study to improve your students' learning process. If you are considering solutions with a particular student, then you can consider a case study.

To write the background of the problem for a case study, you have to focus on the background of that particular child. However, in an action research study, the background generally focuses on an issue with a group of students or with an instructional strategy. The background of the study does not have a set number of words, but it needs to be comprehensive enough to lead to the next section, which is reviewing related literature.

Discussion Questions

1. Why is the background of the problem section important for a research study?

2. How do you envision the steps you will take to write up the background of the problem for your study?

Activities

1. Find a couple of research studies in your subject area and examine how the authors have written the background of the problem section.

2. Use a highlighter to identify the background of the problem in the studies you are examining and write the important points from one of the studies you are examining.

For Your Study

1. Write down some of the problems in your topic.

2. Find citations for and references to the problems that you are addressing.

3. Write down the background of problem for your study.

WRITING THE LITERATURE REVIEW FOR YOUR STUDY, INCLUDING REFERENCES

How to Search for Literature and Research Studies Online

Once you have written the background, now it is time to explore the related literature. The first step is to plug in key words to online search engines and see what you come up with. Make every effort to use more than one database: EBSCOhost, ProQuest, ERIC (EBSCO), Academic Search Premier, ScienceDirect, and Google Scholar are good examples.

Furthermore, look at the descriptors in the subject section from one article to find ideas for keywords. Write down all the possible keywords and then start exploring mixing and matching keywords, a few at a time, to search extensively. Make a folder on the selected database to save all the searches.

If you find a lot of articles, then you need to narrow your search and be more specific with keywords. If you are finding very few articles, then you need to expand your search using other keywords that you have not used yet. You really want to find a good amount of keywords, not too many or not too few. Refer to appendix A, "Guidelines for Writing a Literature Review."

For the purpose of an action research or a case study, you can find articles that relate to similar problems or relate to strategies. For example, if the reading area in your class is not used by your students, then find articles on how to popularize the reading area. If the students are getting disinterested in learning mathematics, then look for strategies other researchers have used. In other words, research what solutions are offered from different studies that you could implement in your classroom to examine the effectiveness of different strategies. Therefore, by reviewing the related literature, you will identify problems related to your field, or you may find strategies to solve these problems.

Grouping Articles and Creating Themes

Once you collect a suitable amount of related literature then it is time for you to group the articles. The first step is to examine the titles and the abstracts of the articles you have gathered.

Next, determine how you will group the articles. To do that, you must create a few categories; four is a good number. These categories become the themes under which the articles will be grouped. My suggestion is to create a Microsoft Word document and write down the name of the categories first and then the titles and authors of the articles you have gathered under each category.

Remember that one article could be placed under more than one category. Also remember that you need at least two articles to place under each category because you need to compare and contrast the main points of the articles. You may also write a few keywords from the title and create themes with the keywords.

Before comparing articles, you will need to create fields. The fields could be article title, purpose, and so on. Table 6.1 lists fields you can use to compare each article.

Next, adjacent to each field try writing the main points of each article. Under each theme that you have created before, you need to compare and contrast articles based on the main points. By compar-

Table 6.1. Comparing Articles

Fields	Article 1	Article 2
1. Title		
2. Author(s)		
3. Year of publication		
4. Purpose		
5. Research question		
6. Sample		
7. Significance		
8. Instruments used		
9. Results		
10. Discussion		
11. Limitation		
12. Implication		

ing articles, you can justify what the related studies have focused on. Then you need to write comments for each article. You can reflect on the article and write a few sentences for each article.

While writing this section, please refer to each article using the author's last name and year of publication. While the full information of the article should be inserted in the reference section at the end, in this section only last names of the author(s) and the year of publication should be included in APA style. No title of the article is necessary here. The comments that you wrote will help you connect the articles from one to the other. Finally, it is also important for you to summarize all the articles based on the theme at this point.

The following is a list of some of YouTube videos that could help you write a literature review.

https://www.youtube.com/watch?v=70n2-gAp7J0
https://www.youtube.com/watch?v=FEhRApOQ_EQ

Discussion Questions

1. Why does a research article need to have a section on literature review?

2. How old or current literature should a research study have?

Activity

1. Find a research article in your subject area and highlight each field.

For Your Study

1. Using a word processor, type up the titles of all the articles that you have gathered for your study, leaving sufficient space between each title to cut them into separate strips of paper. Cut the article titles into separate strips. Take a few boxes (shoe boxes are fine) and write down key terms on the boxes. Each box should be clearly labeled. Determine each article's keywords and place the article in the appropriate box. A title may belong in more than one box, so make copies of the article title to place in each appropriate box. Then it will be easier for you to compare the articles inside each box.

2. Complete the fields from each article (see table 6.1).

3. Compare and contrast the articles based on the fields.

WRITING THE NEED FOR AND SIGNIFICANCE OF YOUR STUDY

Writing the need and significance of your study is very important. Need and significance justifies your study. You will seldom find subheadings stating the *need* and *significance* of a study; however, in most of the studies, need and significance are embedded before an author states the purpose of the study.

The *need* of the study is to fill the gap that exists in the current literature regarding your topic. The need could be a certain area that other researchers have not focused on in their particular studies. In general, studies use specific statements to state the need of the study. Typical needs statements in research include the following:

"Although the above literature mentioned . . ."
"However, there is a limitation in . . ."
"Very few studies have focused on . . ."
"There is limited research found on . . ."

The significance of the study is the importance of the study. Here you have to rationalize why your study is important. Further state what this study will contribute to the field of education. The significance of the study should be very clear in your mind so that you can define it succinctly for the reader.

CHAPTER SEVEN

Discussion Questions

1. Why must research studies state *need* and *significance*?

2. How would you identify a "need" statement in a study?

3. How would you identify the significance of a study?

Activities

1. Find a research study in your subject area and highlight the "need" statement in the study.

2. Use a different color highlighter and highlight the significance of the study.

For Your Study

1. Identify where exactly you should place the "need" statement of your study.

2. Identify where exactly you should place the significance of your study.

3. Write down the "need" statement for your study.

4. Write down the significance of your study.

CHAPTER EIGHT
WRITING THE PURPOSE OF YOUR STUDY AND THE RESEARCH QUESTION

It is absolutely essential to clearly state the purpose of the study and the research question. Although from the start of your study you have an idea of the purpose of your study, this is the place where you need to clearly state the purpose. You already should have briefly mentioned the purpose of your study in the introduction; however, in this section, you will clearly state and explain the purpose of your study. Most research articles specifically state the purpose of the study with the following statement: "The purpose of the study is . . ." In your study, you should have only one or two purposes. The statement explaining the purpose needs to be clear and straightforward. Too many purposes may cause unnecessary complications or may distract the reader.

The research question emerges from the purpose of the study. Since it is a question, you need to end the question with a question mark. Further, each research question should be clearly stated. Each question needs to be answered in the study.

You can try to write the prediction, or research hypothesis, here. Generally, it is appropriate to use the "If . . . then" format to state the research hypothesis, for example, "If the students complete their homework, then their test scores will increase." The null hypothesis is just the reverse, for example, "If the students complete their homework, then their test scores will not increase." My advice is to state the null hypothesis because you do not know until you analyze your data whether you will accept your research hypothesis and reject the null hypothesis or vice versa. The terms *research* or *hypothesis* are generally used in quantitative studies, but these terms help you become focused in your study.

Guidelines for a Research Question

The following are guidelines to help you develop your research question:

1. The question must be one that has not been answered in other research.

2. The question should be open ended.

3. The question should require critical thinking.

4. The question should invoke thought and should have depth.

5. You should be passionate about learning the answer to the question you are proposing.

6. The question should be related to your work.

7. The question should be grounded in "real life" and should be meaningful to you.

8. The question should be stated using simple language. It is better to avoid superlatives.

9. The question should be clear and concise.

10. The question should be answered from a practical point of view.

11. The question should be manageable enough to answer in a timely fashion.

Discussion Questions

1. Why is it important to write the purpose and the research question(s)?

2. Why is it important to have a few (maybe one or two) research questions?

Activity

1. Find a research study in your subject area and identify if there is any hypothesis or prediction stated.

For Your Study

1. Try writing a hypothesis or prediction for your study.

WRITING THE
METHODOLOGY OF YOUR STUDY

Setting

The setting is the first subheading under the methodology section. The setting is the place where you will collect the data. If you plan to collect data in your school, then you can get demographic information from the internet about your school. You can find relevant information about the school's students, such as gender distribution, socioeconomic status, and ethnicity. You can state the general geographic location of your school (e.g., the name of the county and state) and the type of school (e.g., elementary, secondary, vocational, or charter school); however, you must keep the name and address of the school confidential.

Sample

The subjects or the participants of your study are defined as the study "sample." Describe the subjects of your study clearly. First of all, mention the makeup of your sample. Are the subjects your own students? Have the subjects been randomly selected? Have they been selected from an accessible population? Explain in detail how you selected the subjects. Then state how many subjects in total are in the study. If it is an experimental study, then include the subjects in the comparative group as well and state the total number of subjects.

In narrative form, mention in detail all relevant information about the subjects for the study, including gender, socioeconomic status, cultural background, and other information that the readers need to know about the subjects (omit any confidential information). The names of all subjects should be kept anonymous and confidential at all times. You may even use a pseudonym for each participant.

Procedure

The procedure of the study is the step-by-step plan of execution of the study. I would suggest you start writing the procedure from the time you contacted the principal of your school. If you selected some other school, then state why and how you selected the school.

You will need to create a consent form (refer to appendix B) and obtain permission from the school principal before you start collecting data. If the students are minors, then take advice from the principal about how to get permission from the parents. If teachers or other staff are in your sample, then you need to create a consent form for each group and get written consent before administering your research.

If the students are minors, then you need to read the consent form to the students and explain to them that this project is not part of their grades and they can withdraw at any time with no penalty. You should also mention to the students about the purpose of the study and what are your plans after you have collected the data.

Design and Nature

The term *design* in research is defined as the plan about how to proceed. The plan involves determining the setting, sampling other data sources, and examining the research question. It is similar to planning an itinerary when you go on a vacation. You may have an idea about what to see and where to go on your vacation, but you expect to learn the unknown.

If you are a new researcher, it is normal to feel anxious about conducting your first study. The main idea is to develop a plan of who to observe and who to interview. Schedule the interviews so that you can get the answers to your research question. The main consideration is to be practical. You may have to finish the research within a short time frame, perhaps in a semester. Therefore, select a study that you can finish in a reasonable amount of time. Try to focus on a specific problem rather than having scattered ideas. However, in a qualitative research study, it is hard to be very specific.

As a teacher, you want to solve problems that are occurring in your classroom. Be mindful of the ethical issues as a teacher researcher. The purpose of your research is to solely solve the problem in your classroom. Study something that is of interests to you and you feel is important to investigate. However, you should be open and flexible to learn as you continue your research. The following is a list of YouTube videos that will help you in your research process.

https://www.youtube.com/watch?v=WY9j_t570LY
https://www.youtube.com/watch?v=NOD2CZPaVLQ
https://www.youtube.com/watch?v=oNpA-joyuZY

Table 9.1 details a plan for an action research study, including an example.

Instruments

Test instruments are the methods you will use to collect data. In a quantitative study, you need to focus on the dependent variable, which is the outcome variable. Generally, test and quiz scores are examples of dependent variables. Independent variables are factors that may have influence on the dependent variables. Generally, gender

Table 9.1. Plan for an Action Research Study

What	How	Who	When	Where	Resources
Identify the problem	Brainstorm solutions	Sample	Time	Location	Materials
Example: Children are becoming disinterested in mathematics	1. Integrate math with music 2. Integrate math with sports and games	Children Teachers Parents Staff	Morning and afternoon	School(s)	Music devices; sports equipment

(having two levels: male and female), socioeconomic status (having three levels: high, medium, and low) could be independent variables. If you are using an instrument having a Likert-type scale, try to have an even number of choices. You may notice in a five-point scale (1: strongly disagree; 2: disagree; 3: neutral; 4: agree; 5: strongly agree) that participants may choose "3: neutral." Those choices will create difficulty when you analyze your data. Therefore, I suggest that make a scale as (1: strongly disagree; 2: disagree; 3: agree; 4: strongly agree). This will help remove the error of central tendency. You will find another example of a survey questionnaire in appendix C.

In a qualitative study, you will need three separate data sources to triangulate your data. For example, your study could include an open-ended survey questionnaire, focused interview questions, and guided observation.

You must research all test instruments from previous literature. If the instruments are available from previous literature, then you could cite the instrument and state the reliability and validity of the instruments from the same source. If you find a test instrument related to your topic of research, you could take necessary permission to use it in your study and state the reliability and validity. If you find a test instrument but have to modify it to fit the needs of your study, then state the source and mention that you had to modify the instrument according to the study's needs. You may need to buy test instruments or obtain special permission to use them. If you do not find test instruments even after searching various research studies and searching through the internet, then you need to develop the instruments according to your needs. However, you need to state in the limitations section that your instrument was created by the researcher (provide a rationale) and, therefore, reliability could not be established. If you can do a pilot test a few times, then reliability could be established. Reliability is consistency over time. Face or content validity could be established if you show the test instruments to your colleague or your supervisor to find out if it measures what it is supposed to measure.

Data Analysis Method

Data can be analyzed quantitatively or qualitatively. Quantitative analysis should be done using statistics. You can use statistics software such as SPSS, or you can use Microsoft Excel if you do not have access to SPSS.

Qualitative analysis is done through a thematic approach. Data must be grouped according to categories. The following is a list of some YouTube videos that may be helpful:

https://www.youtube.com/watch?v=kuyt0u_tFi4
https://www.youtube.com/watch?v=HFGVJJMDo4I

Guidelines for Your Research Design

First, state your research question. Second, state your major purpose for collecting data. Third, briefly state your method(s) of data collection and how they match your purpose. Finally, address these specific areas:

- Setting: Where will the data be collected?

  - What school? (Don't identify by exact name and location.)

  - What classroom or classrooms? (In your actual paper, you will describe the setting in more detail. For example, you might say: "Grade 2 in an urban elementary school," or "Grade 11 history class in a large high school in the New York metropolitan area.")

- What kinds of data do you plan to collect?

  - What different types of data are you collecting? (For example, state what the strategies the teacher uses; students' responses to questions; student work products from assignments; peer interaction during class time.)

- ○ How will you collect the data? (For example, field notes, audiotape, informal interview.)

- ○ During what activities do you plan to collect data?

• Study participants: Who do you plan to observe, and how/why did you select them?

- ○ State, for example, whether you want to administer to a whole class, to particular children, or to the same teacher in two classes.

- ○ Remember that, in some cases, if you are observing in your own classroom, you will actually be collecting some data on yourself.

• What is your role in the activities?

- ○ Are you an outside observer?

- ○ Do you have a dual role in the classroom as teacher and as researcher?

- ○ If you are the teacher, do you plan to implement an intervention, or do you plan to just observe what "normally" goes on in select situations?

- ○ If you are the teacher, you may be a participant observer.

- ○ As an observer, you will record only what you saw and heard.

- ○ Keep logs of short observations with date and time. Short observations may turn into long logs.

- ○ Try to write up the log on the same day so that you don't forget important details.

- ○ Observe deeply and record your observations seriously.

- ○ Try to be as unobtrusive as possible when writing.

- ○ Videotaping or audiotaping are excellent ways to record interviews.

- ○ Keep your evaluation and comments separate. Keep generous margins for comments.

- How did you gain access to the setting? (State how you obtained permission if you are an outside observer.)

  - ○ Are there any strategies for making data collection easier?

    - ▪ Will a colleague aid in data collection?

    - ▪ What can you do yourself that is not too overwhelming?

- Schedule for collection of data.

  - ○ How often will data be collected?

  - ○ Over how long a period will you collect data?

  - ○ On what days will you collect data? (Some of these answers can be formatted into a separate table.)

- How do you initially plan to analyze the data?

  - ○ Type up your "raw" field notes.

  - ○ Explain the field notes.

  - ○ In preparation for analyzing the data, write a paragraph about possible personal biases:

    - ▪ What do you hope or wish to find?

    - ▪ What do you think you know about your topic?

○ Read through the notes several times and begin to gather your thoughts and code. (For example, look for similarity in the answers and identify patterns.)

Discussion Questions

1. Why do you think your study sample needs to be described at great length?

2. Why is it necessary to write down every step in the procedure section?

3. What sources are you thinking of gathering data from?

Activities

1. Find four research studies in your area and examine how they each described the sample, setting, procedure, and instruments.

2. Compare the sample, setting, procedure, and instruments within the articles and select one article that best relates to your theme.

For Your Study

1. Follow the steps outlined in the "Guidelines for Your Research Design" section of this chapter and answer the questions specifically for your study.

2. Check to see if you have answered all the questions.

CHAPTER TEN
WRITING THE FINDINGS
AND REPORTING RESULTS

In the findings section, you could start by stating the research question here again because it will provide more focus for your study. Then you could mention how you are answering the research question with the help of the instruments. In the findings section, you will detail the results that you found from your data. You will first need to organize and analyze your data.

If you are analyzing data quantitatively, then you have to report using statistics. First, with the help of a table, you report mean and standard deviation or other statistics as needed. This should be followed by graphical representation after each table. Each table or graph should be explained clearly and in detail.

For qualitative analysis, data should be analyzed thematically. The similarities of all the data need to be codified. A simple way to codify is to use different colored highlighters. Use one highlighter for one common feature among all the data. Then use a different highlighter color to identify another common feature among all the data and so on until you find all the commonalities. Each commonality should be grouped and coined a theme. Under the same theme, the differences could also be integrated. Therefore, under each theme, the data have to be compared and contrasted. The comparison could also be demonstrated using a table to help the readers. This section could be very long as it needs to be detailed.

Step-by-Step Instructions to Analyze Your Data

To analyze your data, first review the data gathered from using your test instruments. In this outline, I have used the term *cooked*, which means to give the data time or space to be processed. The following are examples:

1. Field notes: These need to be "cooked" before coding; number the sections that correspond to samples of student work or other artifacts.

2. Tapes: Transcribe tapes of your interviews (both audio and visual columns are needed on the same sheet). For the audio, insert only what's relevant and leave a column for "cooking."

3. Student work: Copy or scan student work with room to "cook"; date the sample and number it so you can pair it with the field notes.

4. Tick sheets: Prepare totals for each page so frequencies are easier to report.

5. Interviews: Practice a few times before indexing or coding.

6. Try indexing.

7. Go back and check over any and all sets of data and "index," or categorize items related to your research questions directly.

8. Index just for one subset. (For example, "teachers' definitions of good work.")

9. Define symbols: Use a symbol to note, for example, when the teacher is revealing his or her definition for good work. You'll notice that even this one search turns out several types of definitions of good work, so you'll have to create sub-symbols or words to code each incident. As examples, a symbol could be an asterisk (*), and a sub-symbol could be a plus (+) sign. Remember you are looking for the sense from your data.

10. Create a "category index": For a sample, see Hubbard and Power (2003, p. 101).

11. Journaling: Write about this process in your research journal to state what sense is beginning to emerge for you about what's going on in this class/setting. What should you be paying more attention to as you continue collecting data related to this discovery?

12. Stop and reflect:
    a) Which instrument is working best to get good data?
    b) If you think your interviews are better than your observations for this setting, what could you do to be a better interpreter of human behavior?
    c) Make sure to check the following: Are you losing data from over-focusing on one source? How can you get better data from another instrument?

13. Coding:
    a) Read through one-quarter of each data set.
    b) Create a name or category for each event that seems related to your research question(s).
    c) For student artifacts, you may want to follow the categories found in your field notes and put all related artifacts in labeled folders.
    d) Find codes by writing yourself "memos" to sort out the categories that are emerging (see Hubbard & Power,

2003, p. 110). What story is the data telling? Tell the whole story.

14. Comparison method of analysis:
    a) What categories are emerging, and what concepts are inherent in these categories?
    b) After you have all your codes, which ones can be collapsed into one another or related to some larger framework mainly from the literature?
    c) After you have most of your data, figure out what your emerging theory is about what's going on. Do all your data confirm this theory?
    d) Try and summarize this theory in your own words.

15. Triangulate the data from all the three sources to compare well:
    a) What three data sources are telling you the same thing about your findings?
    b) Describe how each data set provides a different perspective on the problem.
    c) Make sure to recount these overlaps in your write-up of the findings.

16. Crystalize your findings:
    a) Try to force your interpretation through another medium (e.g., paint a picture, write a poem, or find a metaphor for your findings in the subway, on the bus, in the kitchen, or in art or music).
    b) Do a "free write," build a graphic organizer, or explain your findings to non-education friends.
    c) Articulate clearly what story your data tells.

See table 10.1 for a checklist to help you write your research report.

Table 10.1. Writing a Research Report Checklist

Develop a plan for writing a report for your research study:
1. Identify your intended audience.
2. Identify how to disseminate your findings (e.g., presentations at a conference, writing for a journal).
3. Develop an outline of the major headings and subheadings of your report.
4. Set aside a writing routine with a common time that works best for you.
5. Develop a writing schedule or time line to keep yourself focused to complete the report.
6. Adopt a conversational style of writing as if you are telling a story to a friend.
7. Find a friend who can give you honest feedback and constructive criticism and proofread your work.
8. Revise your report and submit.

Discussion Questions

1. Why do you think it is important for findings to be organized in table format?

2. Why is it necessary to provide graphs after each table?

Activities

1. Find four research articles and examine how the authors have organized the results.

2. Determine which article did best in organizing the results.

For Your Study

1. If your study is quantitative in nature, determine if you will use Microsoft Excel or SPSS.

2. After plugging in the data, check if the program can give you a table and a graph.

3. If your research study is qualitative in nature, determine the common patterns from your data and write them down. These common patterns become the themes. Do the same with the differences under the same theme.

4. Use quotes from your subjects under each theme. Then you can show the similarities in the answers and then connect them later so that the whole write-up has a nice flow from one section to another.

CHAPTER ELEVEN
WRITING THE DISCUSSION OF YOUR STUDY

The discussion of your study has a key role. The discussion explains the results of the study in simple terms, which will captivate the reader's interest. You can refer to the tables from your results section and clarify what the data mean. You must go into detail and explain each table and graph from the results section, taking excerpts from your data.

You then need to state the implication of the study. Mainly from the results, you need to state what this study implies. Further, mention what the readers need to learn from your study.

The next step is to connect the findings of your study with that of the related literature you reviewed previously. Additionally, with the support of your data, you will have to state whether you, as a researcher, agree or disagree with the author(s) from each study that you reported in the literature review. Both similarities and differences should be clearly stated and explained. You can also refer to the themes from the results section.

You then must state all the limitations of the study. Geographical parameters, time constraints, or lack of reliability of the instrument(s), for example, could all be mentioned in the limitations section.

Finally, you need to write about ideas for future study. Describe how this study could be replicated or extended to contribute more to the field of education. This section could be lengthy as it needs to be explained well. The detailed explanation will give your readers a clear understanding of your research.

Discussion Questions

1. What are the main points in the discussion section that you must state in your study?

2. Why is it necessary to use simple language in the discussion section?

Activities

1. Find two new research articles in your subject area and examine how the authors have discussed their studies in their respective discussion sections.

2. State which article has done a good job in explaining the study results. State, without reading the whole study, what you are able to understand about the contribution of the study just by reading the discussion.

For Your Study

1. Write down all the important contributions of your study in simple language.

2. State with which authors your study could be compared and how.

3. What are some of the limitations of your study?

4. What are your ideas of a future study?

CHAPTER TWELVE
WRITING THE
CONCLUSION OF YOUR STUDY

The conclusion is the final section of your study. Generally, it is one brief paragraph that states what the study wanted to find and what was found. In other words, restate the objective or purpose of the study and the findings of the study in a few sentences. Then restate the importance of the study in simple terms and end with the knowledge it has contributed to the field of education.

The conclusion should be written in such a way so that the readers can assess the benefits of your study without reading the whole study. It is a brief paragraph but a powerful one. Readers should get a clear picture of your study if they should choose to read the conclusion ahead of time.

Organizing the Appendixes

The appendixes should be labeled A, B, C, D, and so on. Each appendix should be referred to in the text. The appendixes should include the following components:

Consent forms: Include all the blank consent forms per group of subjects.

Test instruments: Include all the blank test instruments.

Raw data: Include all data with date and time. All names should be erased, and faces of all children in any pictures should be hidden.

Discussion Questions

1. Why do you consider that the conclusion of your study is powerful?

2. What does the conclusion in a study mainly discuss?

Activities

1. Find a new research study in your subject area. Read the conclusion of the study. Write down what you could say about the following:
   a) the purpose of the study
   b) findings of the study
   c) contribution of the study

For Your Study

1. Write the purpose of the study and explain it in one sentence.

2. Write the findings of the study and explain these in a couple of sentences.

3. Write the significance of the study highlighting the contribution to the field of education.

GUIDELINES FOR WRITING A LITERATURE REVIEW

Understanding the Problem

1. What major themes or ways of seeing the problem are emerging in the articles? Organize these on index cards with the full reference information.

2. Organize your literature review by the *themes* you have found, not by the articles and authors (as you would in an annotated bibliography).

3. Label each subsection of the paper with the theme or category that you identified. Use "evidence" from the articles that relate to the theme. Follow that up with your own interpretation of the finding. Connect the finding to your study. Why is this information important to understand for your own proposed study?

4. Your article annotations with summary and comments will help a lot with this process.

Each time you use an article, consider these points:

1. Quickly review the article's purpose, methods, and important findings.

2. Clarify how the article supports your reasoning for choosing the topic of inquiry.

3. Connect it to other articles or ways of seeing the problem.

4. Clarify how the article is helpful in explaining a particular phenomenon.

5. Demonstrate your thinking process to your readers (e.g., choice of article, items you focused on, how you analyzed its usefulness).

6. Indicate the direction (or opposition) with your own proposed study.

Types of Articles

For research, choose both qualitative and quantitative studies. A minimum of 10 (ask your instructor about the requirement) of these research articles should be used (more is better than less in this case). Confirm with your professor the number of articles you need.

"Building" Your Story with Literature

The literature review could be considered analogous to a meeting in a conference room. What is the current discussion that's going on among these informed people?

- Who agrees with whom?

- Who disagrees?

- How does each "team" frame the problem in question?

Tell the tale of what happened in the room, based on your own perspective or way of seeing the problem. Keep in mind that the literature review is just that—an analytical review of scholars' work, not your own opinion. In other words, this section is not appropriate for a reflection paper.

Create a rough outline so that you are clear where your argument is headed. It is always a good idea to make an outline, with the research question clearly stated at the top. This way, you will easily identify the parts of the paper and how to answer the research question when you start to write the actual paper.

Make sure that your literature review looks like a traditional paper. Include an introduction that tells the reader what you plan to do, organize your themes, and use multiple authors (with the last names of the author and year of publication) in your discussions.

Use transitional sentences to get from one article to the next, perhaps noting their similarities or differences. The following are examples of transitional sentences:

"Whereas works of Barrens (2004) and Smith (2006) claim school experiences are a significant predictor of dropout among urban high school students . . ."
"Criss (2005) and Matthews (2007) suggest something different."

Give a brief snapshot of these articles and, most important, analyze them for similarities and differences.

Finally, present a conclusion that links the articles to your research questions and proposed study. At this point, do not reiterate what you already stated in the review. Instead, your purpose is to conclude. You can answer this question: What does your analysis mean?

APPENDIX A

Literature Review Guidelines with an Example

The purpose of a review of the literature is to explore what has been discovered and written about the topic of interest, and then to articulate the nature of the current "conversation" about the topic. The following is an example of a research study title with step-by-step instructions to guide you toward writing the literature review for that study.

Example research study title: What factors contribute to dropout rates among high school students in urban areas?

Step 1: Identify the Keywords in Your Research Question

For this example, I would identify the words *high school*, *urban*, and *dropout*. Enter these keywords in the ERIC (EBSCO) database (use other databases, too, like ProQuest, for example), find articles that relate to your topic, and collect at least 10 articles that help you answer the research question.

Step 2: Read Each Article's Abstract

Determine if the article is based on research or opinion. A research study can be identified by sections such as "methods," "participants," and "results." (Not all articles will designate results, discussion, or conclusions. Be aware of this when reading articles.) Historical and theoretical pieces are often organized in a different manner; they do not use participants but, rather, discuss the issue in a scholarly way. Any article that comes from a peer-reviewed journal can be used for this assignment. If these terms are not in the article—that is, they do not offer evidence from research conducted—you should not include them in the articles used for this assignment.

Step 3: Identify Each Article's Angle

After you have identified the articles that you will use for this assignment, read each article and label it with a sticky note corresponding to its general "angle" or approach to the problem or its conclusion about the problem. After you read a few articles, you will probably begin to see a few categories of information. Examples for the research question might include the following: (a) attitude toward school; (b) experiences in school; (c) amount of time spent earning money; and (d) level of parents' education.

Step 4: Reflect

At this point, you have read enough articles to feel that you are able to "characterize" the "conversation" that is currently going on about your topic. If not, simply go back to the databases and find more articles!

Some questions to address in your reflection:

1. How do the articles frame the current debate about your topic? How do the articles define the problem?

2. How would you categorize the types of solutions they suggest?

3. In what ways are they actually "talking" to each other's work? In other words, how do they talk about how *others* have framed the debate, and what do they suggest in contrast?

4. What are they *not* talking about? In other words, have they ignored different ways of seeing or attending to the problem/issue?

5. How can the knowledge you have gained so far contribute to any new project/research on this issue?

Keep in mind that a literature review does not list each article that relates to the research question. Rather, you will analyze the articles under a heading that answers the research question by comparing and contrasting elements of the articles. This will include a description of each of the elements of the article. For example, with reference to the example research question, I might find two articles that examine students' perceptions of (attitudes toward) school, but one article took a sample from an urban high school and one article used a sample of a rural high school.

Other articles that would fit under this heading might include the attitudes of students who have dropped out of both public and private high schools. Other articles that could be analyzed under this heading may include quantitative studies (that use a large database of information) and qualitative studies (that may use interviews with a few dropouts.) In this section of the literature review, I would describe the participants of the study and how the study was conducted. I would detail the findings and relate (compare and contrast) any or all of that information to the other studies I use in my paper. I would then repeat that process throughout the paper. See appendix G for a rubric to help you evaluate your literature review (table G.1) and a rubric to evaluate your research study (table G.2).

CONSENT FORM TEMPLATE

C heck with the Institutional Review Board (IRB) of your institution regarding policies and protocol of IRB, human subjects review, and template of writing a consent form.

(Letterhead of Your Institution)

Consent to Participate in Research Study

Your school has been invited to take part in a research study to learn more about (title of your research project). This study will be conducted by (your name), of (name of your institution) Department of (name your department) as a part of his/her research study.

The objective of the research study is (state the research objective). I, (your name), will be working as a principal investigator for my study and will be collecting data for the research project. (*State your subjects here.*)

The research project may involve (state clearly details about the project and time frame; state whether the participants will be audiotaped or videotaped).

There are no known risks associated with your participation in this research beyond those of everyday life.

This research may help us understand . . . [*state here how this project will help*].

Confidentiality of the children's research records will be strictly maintained by the principal investigator, (your name). The responses will be kept confidential with the following exception: the researcher is required by law to report to the appropriate authorities if there is any suspicion of harm to the researcher, to children, or to others.

The children's responses will be kept confidential by the researcher.

Participation in this study is voluntary. The children may refuse to participate or withdraw at any time without penalty. The children also have the right to skip or not answer any question if he/she prefers not to answer.

If there is anything about the study or the children's participation that is unclear or that you do not understand, if you have questions or wish to report a research-related problem, you may contact (your name, address, phone numbers and e-mail address) or the Human Subject Review Board (their phone number and e-mail address).

I will participate in this study: _____ (yes/no)

_____   _____   _____
Print name   Signature   Date

Example of Test Instrument— Sample of Survey Questionnaire

Survey Sample

Parenting Sense of Competence Scale

Please rate the extent to which you agree or disagree with each of the following statements.

Strongly Disagree	Somewhat Disagree	Disagree	Agree	Somewhat Agree	Strongly Agree
1	2	3	4	5	6

1. The problems of taking care of a child are easy to solve once you know how your actions affect your child, an understanding I have acquired.

   1   2   3   4   5   6

2. I would make a fine model for a new mother/father to follow in order to learn what she/he would need to know in order to be a good parent.

   1   2   3   4   5   6

3. Being a parent is manageable, and any problems are easily solved.

    1   2   3   4   5   6

4. I meet my own personal expectations for expertise in caring for my child.

    1   2   3   4   5   6

5. If anyone can find the answer to what is troubling my child, I am the one.

    1   2   3   4   5   6

6. Considering how long I've been a mother/father, I feel thoroughly familiar with this role.

    1   2   3   4   5   6

7. I honestly believe I have all the skills necessary to be a good mother/father to my child.

    1   2   3   4   5   6

Teacher Observation Sample

- My informal observations noted that the students were more interested in learning mathematics after they participated in music. Following are the documents with dated clips.

- The students said, "I want to dance some more" and "I like to show my drum and count the beats."

- The students said, "Math is boring," "I don't want to do math," and "Why do we have to learn math?"

- The students also told me verbally, "I like to do math when you play the songs" and "Music helps me learn math better." (This was also reflected in the comments from the survey.)

RESEARCH PAPER OUTLINE

It is expected that each student's paper will take a somewhat different form, depending on the research question. However, here is a broad and somewhat flexible outline.

Outline

- Title page (Include student name, course number, research question, and date.)

- Table of contents (Include page numbers.)

- Research question (This should be in an introductory paragraph with no heading.)

- Rationale for the research question (Explain why it is important to you and to the field; detail how you chose your question; and include your wonderings.)

- Initial literature review (The first draft must synthesize at least four articles.)

  ○ The literature review includes discussion of other researchers' findings that relate to your research question and on which you might build; the review also includes a discussion of important concepts and/or research methods that have been introduced by previous researchers and that are important to your own research.

- The literature review topic headings will depend on your question and what is relevant to your field notes.

- Field investigation

  - Setting

  - Kinds of data I planned to collect

  - Participants

  - Activities that were the focus of data collection

  - My role in the activities

  - Schedule for collection of data

  - Initial plan for data analysis

- Data collection and analysis

  - Ups and downs and ins and outs of the fieldwork process (Include reference to reflective journal/observer comments.)

  - How I analyzed my data

- Findings

  - Examples of what I found

  - Discussion of what I found (and any implications), weaving in some references of other researchers

  - Limitations

  - Further questions (Include what you would investigate further, given more time and resources.)

- Bibliography (This comes at the end of the paper, before the appendix.)

- Appendix

  ○ The appendix includes a sample of raw field notes, samples of different types of data collected, samples of data analysis ("cooking" notes or coding), and excerpts from a reflective journal.

Length and Format of Your Paper

Your research paper should be in APA style, about 20 pages in length, double-spaced, in 12 point font (Times New Roman is recommended), with margins no wider than 1.25 inches on the sides and 1 inch on the top. The title page, table of contents, bibliography, and appendixes are not included in the 20 pages. Number the pages.

Additional Resources

See table D.1 for a research paper checklist and table D.2 for a slide presentation outline.

Table D.1. Final Research Report Checklist

Introduction and context	Have you set the context by describing your school and your class?
	Have you shared why you chose to do this research?
	How does this project contain potential to address school reform issues?
	Why is it necessary for others to know about your study?
Research question	Have you clearly stated your concern in question form and the sub-questions needed to address it?
Literature review/rationale	What literature is needed to understand this problem better?
	How did the literature you have reviewed help you plan your teacher research project?
	How did the articles relate to your context, your classroom, your data collection method, and/or your question?
	What about the literature makes your project necessary for others to know about?

(continued)

APPENDIX D

Table D.1. *(continued)*

Methods	How did you do this study?
	• Describe how you gained access to the site.
Note: Attach your instruments in labeled appendixes.	• Describe each data set (gather from your instruments—interviews, documents, observations, etc.). Why did you choose each data set?
	• What will you be looking for in the answers from each instrument?
	• How long was each instrument used?
	• If informal interviews, who participated? How many students (include gender, age, and ethnicity), teachers, or other staff gave interviews?
	• What kind of ethical issues came up or were involved? How did your own bias, values, or preconceived notions influence your data collection?
	• How did you go about analyzing the data? (Cite the readings to help explain.)
	Reflect on the process of data collection:
	• Were the instruments used effective?
	• How did (or did not) the instruments elicit the data to match your research question?
	• How did you triangulate your results?
	• Why did you choose this methodology?
	• What are its strengths and limitations?
Findings	Organize your major findings into three themes; include subthemes if necessary.
	Introduce each theme, support with data, analyze the data, and support the analysis with literature if needed.
Conclusions	Make sense of your findings:
	• What did you discover about the phenomena in question?ˈ
	• How well did you answer your research questions?
	• Why is this all important?
	• What should we do from here?
	• Reflect on the process of teacher research.
Extras	Make sure to have your paper proofread for grammar and readability.
Note: Attach appendixes (e.g., sample field notes and other data artifacts).	

Table D.2. Outline for a Slide Presentation

Slide 1
Title
Your name
Research report
Date

Slide 2
Introduction (state in one sentence what the problem is and its significance)

Slide 3
Background of the problem
• List the problems in bullet form

Slide 4–11 (as many as needed; roughly 11 slides)
Article 1: Important points, cite author's last name and year of publication wherever needed.
What did the researcher want to find? What was the study sample, procedure, and so on?
What did the researcher find?

Slide 12
Summary of all the articles: Compare and contrast; discuss the main points.

Slide 13
Need (other studies found; what is yet to find; identify the gap)
Significance of the study: Why is the study so important?

Slide 14
Purpose: What is this study about?

Slide 15
Hypothesis or prediction: What do you hope to find? (This slide is optional. You don't need it if you are doing a qualitative study.)

Slide 16
Sample
Procedure

Slide 17
Design
Instruments

Slide 18
Method of data analysis
Is the study qualitative, quantitative, or mixed? Explain the nature of the study.

(continued)

61

Table D.2. *(continued)*

___

Slide 19
Findings
Results
Take each hypothesis and answer each question.
Insert tables/graphs and briefly explain each.

Slide 20
Discussion
Discuss the main points from your findings in simple terms.
Mention how you agree or disagree with other authors from your literature review
    with respect to your study.

Slide 21
Implication in the classroom

Slide 22
Limitations
Ideas for future studies

Slide 23
Conclusion
State the importance of your study again.

Slide 24
References in APA style.

___

GUIDELINES FOR WRITING A CASE STUDY ON A CHILD

S tart working on your child study from the beginning of the semester. Do not state the name of the child or the school as this information is confidential. Document all the observations like running records, anecdotes, narrative event sampling, checklists, and rating scales with dates and approximate time if possible.

Remember that, with all the labeling and categorizing, our goal is still never to lose sight of the whole child.

Outline

1. Introduction

   • Provide school location, grade level, child selected, and age of child (years, months).

   • Provide date you first began observing the child.

   • Explain your role in that child's classroom (e.g., teacher, assistant teacher, visiting observer).

   • Detail how often and for how long you will be at the setting if you are not employed there.

- Include a brief description of the physical setup of the classroom; describe what personal space the child has in this classroom (e.g., a cubby or an assigned seat).

- Include a brief description of the program in this classroom, particularly in terms of the balance of individual, small-group, and whole-group activity, and opportunities for the child to interact with the teacher and with peers.

- Explain what made you originally select this child.

2. Review related literature

   - Enter keywords and find research literature related to your topic.

   - Find the purpose and findings from each article.

   - Write a summary comparing and contrasting the related literature.

3. Scope and organization of observations and other data

   - Include a complete log of your observations. Log includes date of observation, type of observation, time/activity, and a brief note to remind you of what you found out. You must have a minimum of 15 logs, spaced over the semester.

   - Include a one-paragraph summary statement about your entire log, stating what kinds of observation methods you used, what types of activities/settings you observed, and what times of day. This statement should clearly show that you observed the child at a variety of times of day in a variety of situations.

   - Create a pie chart at mid-semester to see just where the gaps were in your observations.

- Describe your system for keeping your observations organized.

- Describe other ways that you have gathered data.

4. Analysis and write-up of your observations

   - Analyze your observations using four developmental domains: cognitive (including language and/or creativity), social, emotional, and physical.

   - Write about the child in each developmental domain, using dated "clips" from your observations as evidence to back up your statements about the child's interests, development, and learning. Write about patterns you have noted or any changes over time. You may also include photos and work products and analyze those.

   - Analyze other ways you have gathered data and report them. End this section with a summary of what you have learned from the analysis including the following:

     ○ A statement about the strengths you have discovered in the child.

     ○ Areas of development that do not meet the developmental milestones or your expectations. You must include a reference to something you have read about developmental stages or milestones.

5. Conclusion

   - What more would you like to know about the child in school?

   - What other sources of information about the child aside from your own observations (e.g., school records, discussion with parents or colleagues) were available to you, and how were they helpful to you, if at all?

6. Recommendation and evaluation

- Write a recommendation for the child.

- If you were responsible for planning for this child, explain one way your analysis might help you set up a planning goal. Be specific.

See appendix G (table G.4) for an example of a rubric to help you evaluate your case study.

ASSIGNMENTS TO COMPLETE THE RESEARCH STUDY

Assignment 1: Topics

1. Brainstorm five topics that you wonder about and write them down. The topics could be from your teaching experience:

_____

_____

_____

_____

_____

_____

2. Prioritize the topics and write them down:

_____

_____

_____

_____

_____

_____

Assignment 2: Keywords

Write down five keywords for each topic:

_____

_____

_____

_____

_____

Assignment 3: Related Literature Search

1. With the keywords, search literature using at least three search engines (e.g., EBSCOhost, ProQuest, Google).

   How many articles have you come across from each search engine? (Remember you don't want too many, nor too few. You want to be somewhere in the middle.) If you get a lot of articles, then narrow down the keywords and make the search more specific. If you get very few, then broaden your search. If you have difficulty, then check the descriptors in a few research articles and do another search.

2. Select roughly 50 research articles and bookmark these in your computer.

Assignment 4: Review of the Literature

1. Detail what problem(s) you will address in your literature review:

_____

_____

_____

2. List specific electronic databases:

_____

_____

_____

3. What key words did you use?
   a. _____
   b. _____
   c. _____
   d. _____
   e. _____
   f. _____

4. What topics and subtopics emerged about your problem and question as you conducted your research? (These could be developed as themes.)

_____

_____

_____

Assignment 5: Scroll through Each Article

Check the following for each article:

1. If this is a research article, do you have distinct subheadings like "methodology" and "findings"?

2. Is the article relevant to your topic?

Assignment 6: Select Articles

Select and bookmark between 20 and 30 articles on your computer.

Assignment 7: Print Out the Relevant Articles

Check with your instructor the number of articles required.

Assignment 8: Group Articles according to Keywords Used in the Articles

1. Use different colored highlighters and write a key to the groups made.

2. Convert the keywords to themes. See table F.1 for a template.

Table F.1. Keywords and Themes

Keywords/Theme	Title of the Article	Author's Last Name	Year of Publication

3. Create 10 bullets and complete table F.2 for all the articles. You may start one article at a time.

Table F.2. Article Fields

Fields	Article 1	Article 2
1. Title		
2. Author(s)		
3. Year of publication		
4. Purpose		
5. Research question		
6. Sample		
7. Significance		
8. Instruments used		
9. Results		
10. Discussion		
11. Limitation		
12. Implication		

Assignment 9: Write a Summary and a Comment

1. Write a summary and a comment in narrative form for each article. See table F.3 for a template.

Table F.3. Summary and Comment

	Article 1	Article 2
Summary		
Comment		

2. Write a conclusion based on the findings of your review:

_____

_____

_____

Assignment 10: References

1. Write citations in APA style in the text.

2. Write complete references for each article at the end.

Assignment 11: Summary of All Articles

Write a summary of all articles based on the themes that you created:

_____

_____

_____

_____

APPENDIX F

Assignment 12: Write the "Need" of the Study

Write about the gap that exists in the literature in your topic:

_____

_____

_____

Assignment 13: Write the "Significance" of Your Study

Justify the importance for investigating this question/problem:

_____

_____

_____

_____

_____

Assignment 14: Write the Purpose of Your Study

_____

_____

Assignment 15: Research Question

1. The research problem is:

_____

_____

2. My research question(s) is/are:

_____

_____

3. Following are the keywords in the problem or question that are not clear and therefore need to be defined:
   a. _____
   b. _____
   c. _____
   d. _____
   e. _____
   f. _____

4. Write the definitions of these words and explain them:

_____

_____

_____

_____

Assignment 16: Write the Introduction

The introduction should start with the problem and end with a purpose (one paragraph):

_____

_____

_____

_____

Assignment 17: Check for Theorist(s) to Follow

_____

_____

Assignment 18: Research Method

1. The specific method(s) that seem(s) most appropriate for me to use at this time is/are (circle all you think are appropriate); give reasons for your choices:
   a. ethnography
   b. correlational study
   c. causal-comparative study
   d. case study
   e. historical study
   f. action research or teacher research study
   g. program evaluation

2. The nature of the research I am thinking is (circle one):
   a. quantitative
   b. qualitative
   c. mixed method

3. State the reason for this nature of research:

_____

_____

_____

_____

_____

_____

Assignment 19: Ethics in Research

1. My research question is:

_____

_____

_____

_____

2. The possibilities for harm to participants (if at all) are
   as follows:

_____

_____

_____

_____

_____

I would address these problems and solve them as follows:

_____

_____

_____

_____

3. The possibilities of problems of confidentiality (if any)
   are as follows:

_____

_____

_____

_____

_____

I would address these problems and solve them as follows:

_____

_____

_____

_____

4. Check your university guidelines on IRB. State your understandings here:

_____

_____

_____

_____

5. Develop a consent form. Check the template in appendix B.

Assignment 20: Design of the Research Study (Quantitative/Qualitative/Mixed)

1. My research question is:

_____

_____

_____

_____

2. If my research is quantitative, my hypothesis is:

_____

_____

_____

_____

3. The variables in my research are:

   a. Dependent _____

   b. Independent _____

4. Possible extraneous variables that might affect my results could be as follows:

   a. _____

   b. _____

   c. _____

5. My research is qualitative or mixed methods. The proposition(s) is/are:

_____

_____

_____

_____

Assignment 21: Plan for Sample

1. The participants in my study consist of (state who and how many). Explain your sample:

_____

_____

_____

2. The demographics (characteristics) of the sample are as follows (e.g., age range, sex, distribution, ethnic breakdown, socioeconomic status, location [where are these subjects located?]):

_____

_____

_____

3. State how the sample is selected (e.g., convenience, purposive, random, stratified random) and state the reason of selecting the sample this way:

_____

_____

_____

4. I will reach my sample through the following steps:

_____

_____

_____

5. External validity:
   a. If results are not generalizable, why not?

   _____

   b. How could you generalize the results of your study. Explain:

   _____

Assignment 22: Test Instruments

1. Describe the types of instrument(s) you plan to use for your research (e.g., survey, interview, test scores, observation scale, questionnaire, etc.). State the reason:

_____

_____

2. Is it a preexisting instrument from other research studies or one you plan to develop? You must search for test instruments in your topic. Summarize what you found:

3. If preexisting, state the name of the instrument:

4. What is the instrument supposed to measure?

5. How many items will the instrument contain?

6. How will the instrument be scored?

Assignment 23: Validity and Reliability of the Test Instruments

1. If it's an existing instrument, report the validity and reliability of scores obtained with this instrument.

2. If you plan to *develop* an instrument, explain how you will try to ensure the validity and reliability of results

obtained with this instrument. If not, then report that in the limitation section of your study.

_____

_____

_____

3. You can check for content validity by asking your colleagues or your supervisor to review your instruments. Who did you ask? (No names are required; state only the positions.)

_____

_____

_____

Assignment 24: Internal Validity

1. Place an X after any of the threats as listed below that you apply to your study:

Subject characteristics   _____

Instrumentation   _____

Maturation   _____

Mortality   _____

Testing   _____

History   _____

Subject attitude   _____

Implementation   _____

Location   _____

Other   _____

2. Please describe how you will attempt to control for those threats:

_____

_____

_____

Assignment 25: Research Methodology

1. The question of my study is:

_____

_____

_____

2. The hypothesis (optional) of my study is:

_____

_____

_____

3. The methodology I plan to use is:

_____

_____

_____

4. Describe the data collection process. When, where, and how will you collect the data?

_____

_____

_____

Assignment 26: Tools

1. If quantitative, what statistics you are using?

_____

2. If qualitative, how do you plan to report the findings?

_____

Assignment 27: Coding

If qualitative, use colored highlighters and check for patterns in the answer. List the patterns:

_____

_____

_____

Assignment 28: Reporting Results

Develop tables and graphical representation (e.g., bar graph, line graph, pie chart).

Assignment 29: Discussion

Report the main points for the discussion section:

_____

_____

_____

_____

Assignment 30: Implication

State the implications of your study:

_____

_____

_____

_____

Assignment 31: Limitations

State the limitations of your study:

_____

_____

_____

_____

Assignment 32: Future Studies

State the ideas for future studies:

_____

_____

_____

_____

RUBRICS FOR EVALUATION

Evaluating a Literature Review Based on a Rubric

1. The level of *understanding* of the studies and their conclusions: Did you understand the study? Did you communicate that understanding well and in your own words?

2. The level of *analysis:* Are there linkages between the studies in the review? Did you articulate the role each study may play in clarifying the field or current conversation about your topic?

3. The level of *synthesis:* Did you find a link between the study's implications and your own thinking about the issue?

4. The *originality* of the work: Is your review unique in the joining together of these particular studies as a lens through which we can understand the problem better?

5. The level of *justification*: To what extent did your exploration of the literature lead to a unique take on the problem at hand and help *justify* your study?

See table G.1 for the accompanying rubric to help you evaluate a literature review.

Table G.1. Rubric for a Literature Review

	Exceeds	4	Meets	2–3	Aspires	0–1	Total
Understanding	The author describes studies and findings in an eloquent and articulate manner.		The author describes studies and findings his or her own words. The presentation is clear.		The author provides basic descriptions, but the review may read more like an annotated bibliography.		
Analysis	All analysis questions are addressed, and there is a clear sense of the "conversation" going on around the topic.		Most analysis questions are addressed, and the set of readings is well explored.		Few analysis questions are addressed. The studies are reported but not analyzed.		
Synthesis	Connections between the body of literature and the author's own study are made clearly and uniquely.		The gathered understandings are related to the author's own study.		A connection between the literature and the author's own study is not made clear.		
Originality	The method of assembling themes is unique and needed in the field. Readers can understand the problem better.		The assembly of themes is present and clearly made by the author.		The lens through which we should be seeing the issue is made by the literature but not by the author.		
Justification	There is a clear justification for the author's own study after reading the review of literature.		There is mention of a direction for the author's own research, but a stronger justification could be made.		There appears to be no justification for the author's own study.		

Evaluating a Research Study

See table G.2 for a rubric to help you evaluate a research study.

Table G.2. Rubric for Evaluating Research

Criteria or Component to Evaluate	(0) Unacceptable/Not Submitted	(1) Inadequate/ Unsatisfactory	(2) Passing/Basic	(3) Good/Proficient	(4) Excellent/Professional
			Level of Performance		
1. Statement of problem, context, and rationale for study	Rationale and problem are missing; no context for study provided.	Rationale and/ or problem are not apparent; some context is provided but is haphazard.	Context is provided but rationale for the problem and/ or study context are not clear.	Context is provided adequately; rationale for the problem is clear.	Thoroughly sets the stage for the study; provides compelling rationale for the work; clearly establishes the problem.
2. Review of literature	Review of literature is missing.	Analysis is poor; no relevance of literature review to study context; review is disjointed.	Analysis of individual articles is adequate but little relevance of literature review to study context; no connections made between studies; writer's voice is unclear.	Analysis is adequate; literature review is relevant to study context; few connections are made among studies.	Analysis of articles and among articles is extensive; literature review is relevant to study context; writer's voice is clear.

Criteria					
3. Design and methods of the study	Methods and design sections are missing.	Methods section is not completed; plan is not fleshed out or poor attention to instrumentation; not informed by course readings.	Design elements are missing; not well aligned with research questions; plan is not clear or instruments will not collect the needed data; weakly informed by course readings.	Methodology is sufficient but not fully explained; adequate instruments to collect data; informed by course readings but still some clarity lacking.	Methodology clearly aligns with research focus and context; contains all design elements; instruments are appropriate to collect all data and are well designed; clearly informed by course readings.
4. Analysis and findings of the study	Findings section is missing.	Little support for findings with data; findings are unconvincing and poorly organized; field notes are poor or missing.	Minimal understanding of the research process; findings are weakly supported by data; appendixes are attached but underutilized; field notes and/or instrumentation are present.	Reflects some understanding of research process; findings are organized and somewhat supported by data; appendixes are attached; field notes and/or instrumentation are present.	Reflects clear understanding of research process; findings extensively supported by data; findings coherent and very well organized; research question is thoroughly addressed; appendixes are extensive and well used; field notes and/or instrumentation are excellent.

(continued)

Table G.2. (continued)

Criteria or Component to Evaluate	(0) Unacceptable/Not Submitted	(1) Inadequate/ Unsatisfactory	(2) Passing/Basic	(3) Good/Proficient	(4) Excellent/Professional
				Level of Performance	
5. Writing conventions and APA style	Writing is unacceptable; parts of the paper are missing.	Writing is poor; paper contains many mistakes and faulty citations; APA format, headings, and citations are poor or missing.	Paper is somewhat disorganized; APA format is inconsistent; citations are improper or incomplete; some headings are used; quality of grammar, syntax, and punctuation is inconsistent; quoting is excessive.	Paper is organized and mostly coherent; good use of APA; grammar, syntax, and punctuation is acceptable; incorporates quotes somewhat appropriately; headings are used satisfactorily.	Writing is comprehensive and cohesive with excellent grammar, syntax, and punctuation; citations are used accurately; headings are used appropriately; APA is current; "voice" is clear.
6. Discussion; implications for teaching practice	Implications and connections to teaching practice are missing.	"So what?" may be missing; little connection to practice; implications are minimally discussed or explored.	"So what?" is not clear; connections back to practice, literature, and real world are minimal but clear; reflection is weak;	"So what?" is clear; good connection to practice and real-world contexts; some connections to literature; implications and	Thoughtful discussion; excellent connection to real-world context; connects back to literature and to practice; implications for

		implications for teaching are not fully explored.	reflection are explored.	further practice are helpful; reflection is compelling.
7. Recommendations and implications for future research and practice	No recommendations or implications provided for future study; no evidence of behavior shown in extending ways to seek information and learning to learn; no critical statement regarding the limitations of the research investigation.	Poorly developed ideas for recommendations and implications are provided; minimal evidence of disposition and/or skills in ways to seek information on own and learning to learn; inadequate, almost no critical statement regarding the limitations of the research investigation.	Some exploration of recommendations and implications for future research and practice; some evidence of addressing ways to seek information on own and learning how to learn; some critical statements regarding the limitations of the research investigation.	Fairly well-developed evidence of transferring discussion, recommendations, and implications to future investigations and new contexts; clear evidence of seeking ways to learn information on own; fairly well-developed critical statements regarding the limitations of the research investigation.	Well-developed evidence revealed of transferring findings, discussion, recommendations, and implications to future investigations and new contexts; reveals high competency in ways to seek and learn information on own in order to conduct future projects; well-developed critical statement regarding limitations of the research investigation.

FINAL EVALUATION

This rubric was created by the School of Education, St. John's University.

Evaluating a Final Report

See table G.3 for a rubric to help you evaluate a final report.

Table G.3. Rubric for a Final Report

Component	Weight	C Work	B Work	A Work
Introduction and context	5%	Addressed few of the guidelines; evidence of reading is absent.	Addressed most of the guideline questions with adequate detail; evidence of reading is weak.	Addressed guideline questions fully and thoughtfully; tightly connected to the reading's recommendations.
Research question	Provided			
Methods	5%			
Review of literature	20%			
Findings	15%			
Conclusions	5			
Extras	+ or -			
Grammar, syntax, flow, appendixes, field notes				

Evaluating a Case Study

See table G.4 for a rubric to help you evaluate a case study.

Table G.4. Case Study Rubric

Criteria or Component to Evaluate	Level of Performance				
	(0) Unacceptable/ Not Submitted	(1) Inadequate/ Unsatisfactory	(2) Passing/Basic	(3) Good/Proficient	(4) Excellent/Professional
1. Communication: Audience Writes professionally for administrators, other professionals, teachers, and parents)	Does not address audiences necessary for task (teachers, parents, others).	Partially addresses some audience members but professional discussion not connected to task.	Generally addresses intended audience with some lapses in clarity and professional language.	Addresses well-defined audience thoughtfully, clearly, and professionally.	Addresses well-defined audience with compelling purpose and clarity in skillful, professional language.
2. Mechanics, grammar, and usage	Inappropriate and inconsistent awareness of conventional grammar and mechanics.	Inconsistently correct grammar and mechanics.	Consistently correct grammar and mechanics.	Consistently correct grammar and mechanics, with varied word choice and sentence structure.	Consistently correct grammar and mechanics, with creative word choice and sentence structure.

(continued)

Table G.4. *(continued)*

	Level of Performance				
Criteria or Component to Evaluate	(0) Unacceptable/ Not Submitted	(1) Inadequate/ Unsatisfactory	(2) Passing/Basic	(3) Good/Proficient	(4) Excellent/Professional
3. Data presentation	Insufficient data presentation.	Inaccurate and/ or inappropriate data presentation.	Adequate data presented and appropriately scored.	Ample data presented and accurately scored and interpreted.	Extensive data presented and accurately scored and interpreted to make a case.
4. Provides background and educational history	No client background and educational history.	Inadequate/minimal client background information; critical gaps.	Basic background/ history outlined.	Plentiful or ample description of background/ history; presented thoughtfully.	Extensive background/ history described professionally to make a case.
5. Analysis	No analysis offered.	Inadequate analysis based on insufficient data.	Basic analysis based on insufficient data.	Analyzes thoughtfully based on sufficient data.	Analyzes thoroughly based on sufficient data.
6. Recommendations; plan of instruction; teaching methodology	No recommendations or plan of instruction offered.	Minimal or inappropriate lesson recommendations offered; no coordinated plan.	Adequate lesson recommendations offered for the plan.	Thoughtful but not comprehensive lesson recommendations; alignment of plans not coordinated with hypothesis.	Comprehensive and creative; in-depth recommendations offered in a plan aligned powerfully with the diagnostic hypothesis.

This rubric was created by the School of Education, St. John's University.

94

Evaluating Oral Presentations

See table G.5 for a rubric to help you evaluate a presentation of the final research report.

Table G.5. Rubric for a Final Research Report Presentation

Criteria or Component to Evaluate	(1) Inadequate/ Unsatisfactory	(2) Passing/Basic	(3) Good/Proficient
1. Visuals	Showed no visual.	Showed some visuals to understand the research.	Showed excellent visuals to understand the research.
2. Presentations	Showed clear and concise presentation of research question(s); methodology and preliminary findings were not clear.	Showed clear and concise presentation of research question(s) and methodology; preliminary findings were not clear.	Showed clear and concise presentation of research question(s), methodology, and preliminary findings.
3. Ability to answer questions from the attendees	Did not answer the questions that the attendees asked; did not engage the audience.	Answered all the questions the attendees asked; did not engage the audience.	Confidently answered all the questions the attendees asked; engaged the audience well.

REFERENCES

Bachman, L. (2001). *Review of the agricultural knowledge system in Fiji: Opportunities and limitations of participatory methods and platforms to promote innovation development* (Unpublished dissertation). Humboldt University of Berlin, Germany. Retrieved from http://citeseerx.ist.psu .edu/viewdoc/download?doi=10.1.1.173.4494&rep=rep1&type=pdf

Coghlan, David, and Mary Brydon-Miller, eds. (2014). *The Sage encyclopedia of action research*. London: Sage. Retrieved from https:// books.google.com/books?hl=en&lr=&id=hNfSAwAAQBAJ&oi= fnd&pg=PP1&dq=Lewin,+K.+(2007).+Action+research+spiral.+ In+Encyclopedia+of+Informal+Education.&ots=LoJFZaGWfx&-sig=2KW7ucDb0VedrVMt-tA3N5JBCPU#v=onepage&q&f=false

Falk, B., & Blumenreich, M. (2005). *The power of questions: A guide to teacher and student research*. Portsmouth, NH: Heinemann.

Glanz, J. (2006). *Fundamentals of educational research: A guide to completing a master's thesis*. Lanham, MD: Rowman & Littlefield.

Hittleman, D. R., & Simon, A. J. (2006). *Interpreting educational research: An introduction for consumers of research* (4th ed.). Upper Saddle River, NJ: Merrill Prentice Hall.

Houghton, P. M., & Houghton, T. J. (2009). *APA: The easy way!* (2nd ed.). Flint, MI: Baker College.

Hubbard, Ruth S., & Power, B. M. (2003). *The art of classroom inquiry: A handbook for teacher-researchers* (Rev. ed.). Portsmouth, NH: Heinemann.

REFERENCES

Johnson, A. P. (2009). *What every teacher should know about action research.* Upper Saddle River, NJ: Pearson.

Johnson, A. P. (2008). *A short guide to action research* (3rd ed.). Boston: Allyn & Bacon.

McMillan, J. H., & Wergin, J. F. (2010). *Understanding and evaluating educational research* (4th ed.). Upper Saddle River, NJ: Pearson.

McMillan, J. H., & Wergin, J. F. (2006). *Understanding and evaluating educational research* (3rd ed.). Upper Saddle River, NJ: Pearson.

Mertler, C. A. (2017). *Action research: Improving schools and empowering educators* (5th ed.). Thousand Oaks, CA: Sage.

Mills, G. E. (2017). *Action research: A guide for the teacher researcher* (6th ed.). Upper Saddle River, NJ: Pearson.

Mills, G. E. (2011). *Action research: A guide for the teacher researcher* (4th ed.). Boston: Pearson.

MSED Research Course Committee. (2014). *MSED handbook for action research.* Charleston: Eastern Illinois University. Retrieved from https://thekeep.eiu.edu/cgi/viewcontent.cgi?referer=https://www.google.com/&httpsredir=1&article=1048&context=eiunca_assessment_docs

Parsons, R. D., & Brown, K. S. (2002). *Teacher as reflective practitioner and action researcher.* Belmont, CA: Wadsworth / Thomson Learning.

Riel, M. (2007). *Understanding collaborative action research.* Center for Collaborative Action Research. Retrieved from http://base.socioeco.org/docs/center_for_collaborative_action_research.pdf

Rowntree, D. (2004). *Statistics without tears: A primer for non-mathematicians.* (Classic ed.). Upper Saddle River, NJ: Pearson Education.

Stake, R. E. (2006). *Multiple case study analysis.* New York: Guilford.

Stringer, E. T. (2014). *Action research* (4th ed.). Thousand Oaks, CA: Sage.

Stringer, E. T. (2007). *Action research* (3rd ed.). Thousand Oaks, CA: Sage.

Yin, R. K. (2018). *Case study research and applications: Design and methods.* Thousand Oaks, CA: Sage.

Yin, R. K. (2014). *Case study research design and methods* (5th ed.). Thousand Oaks, CA: Sage.

INDEX

Page numbers in *italics* refer to tables.

research study evaluation, *88–91*

sample and sampling: assignments for, 77–78; children in studies, 28, 38, 45, 53–54, 63; consent forms, 28, 45, 53–54; describing in methodology section, 27–28, 38; survey questionnaires, 55–56
settings for action research, 27, 32. *See also* permission from school
significance of the study, 21, 72
single case study, xxi
slide presentation outline, *61–62*
SPSS, 32
statistics, 32, 37, 82
Stringer, E. T., xix
student work, 38
subjects of the study. *See* sample and sampling
survey questionnaires, 55–56
symbols, 39

tables for statistics, 37
thematic approach: to literature review, 18–19, *19*, 47–48, 70; in qualitative analysis, 32, 37–38
theoretical perspective, xxi, xxv–xxvi, 74
tick sheets, 38
title of research study, 7–8
topic for research study, 67. *See also* research question
transcription of tapes, 38
transitional sentences, 49
treatment groups, xxv
triangulation of data, *xxii*, 31, 40

validity of instruments, 31, 79–81
variables, 29, 31, 77

websites, 4

YouTube videos: for data analysis, 32; for design of research study, 29; for literature review, 19; for research overview, 2

ABOUT THE AUTHOR

Smita Guha is an associate professor at St. John's University in the School of Education, in the Department of Curriculum and Instruction. She received her PhD from the State University of New York at Buffalo. Her research focuses on teacher education in childhood and early childhood levels, particularly in the areas of mathematics and science education.

She has previously written two books: *Today's Youth, Tomorrow's Leaders: How Parents and Educators Can Influence and Guide the Learning Process* and *Healthy Children: How Parents, Teachers and Community Can Help to Prevent Obesity in Children*. Her articles have been published in peer-reviewed scholarly journals. She has presented at numerous conferences at international, national, state, and regional levels.

She has more than 10 years of experience working directly with children and more than 23 years of experience teaching in higher education.

She has been teaching research courses at her university for about 16 years During her experience in mentoring teachers in the research process, she felt an urge to write this guidebook to help teachers become active researchers. Recently, one of her action research studies and another case study have been published.